THE STARS THAT TWINKLED HOPE

AND OTHER POEMS

Composed by me for you
to encourage a smile!

ANGELA WIGNALL

Published by New Generation Publishing in 2021

First Edition

ISBN: 978-1-80369-056-8

www.newgeneration-publishing.com

New Generation Publishing

For my friends
and family.

Especially for our son Alex
who has given us an abundance
of smiles!

I didn't know what I should do
with all the poems
I wrote for you.

So I decided to put them in this book
and I think it's time
for you to have a look!

Sending sparkles
your way!

angela

23/11/2022

I would like to give special thanks to Florence Lane for all the beautiful illustrations in this book and also the cosmic front cover!

A good friend of mine suggested that her daughter Florence may like to do the illustrations for me, as she had just graduated after working hard to gain a degree in Animation.

I was so lucky Florence had the time to help me. I described to her my thoughts on each illustration and sent her the relevant poems to give her a feel for the drawing. We had a great connection, as every drawing she sent to me, was almost exactly how I had imagined it would be.

She was very professional in that each illustration was ready on time and she was always happy to make any alterations for me to make it perfect! We both thoroughly enjoyed the whole process.

Florence produced the drawings digitally using watercolours. You can find her work on Instagram using @pastelpumpkinstudios

INTRODUCTION

There are over sixty poems in this little book, mostly composed by me, but there is also a lovely selection from family and friends who have been inspired to put pen to paper themselves.

The poems are generally in date order, but there are some exceptions, where I felt the poem should be included with others relaying a similar message.

I believe all the poems have a loving energy within them, because they were composed with the intention of helping the human race in a Cosmic Quest To Heal Planet Earth!

Your mission, should you accept it, is to join that Quest!

THE POEMS

THE COSMIC QUEST TO HEAL PLANET EARTH

THE STARS THAT TWINKLED HOPE AND THE HEAVENLY TEAM

"LOCKDOWN" RHYMES

MORE POEMS

DO YOU BELIEVE IN FAIRIES?

DO YOU BELIEVE IN DRAGONS?

EVEN MORE POEMS

POEMS COMPOSED BY FRIENDS AND FAMILY

THE UNIVERSE

I love writing poetry for family and friends and have been scribbling away for years, making them laugh with entertaining verses, especially for them.

After 2010 and the loss of our dearly loved daughter, Jessica, the poems became more spiritual, but it wasn't until 2017 that I started to write about our planet and how we humans weren't treating it with enough kindness or respect. It was around this time that I wrote the poem *Peace On Earth – Our Future.*

In May 2019 I had just finished a short but enjoyable solitary walk in the forest and was heading to my favourite café for a coffee and a cake. (The thoughts of eating cake bringing delicious and happy memories). I was day dreaming about how clever Mother Nature is to organise such an abundance of beauty for us, when the thought came into my head that Nature was calling to us through a whisper on the breeze, asking us for help.

As I walked to the café, I started to think of the words to a poem and I knew that I was supposed to share the poem with all my friends. I sat down at my favourite little table, ordered my cake and wrote the poem *A Whisper On The Breeze.*

The first few poems in this book are concerned with a quest to heal our planet and how our positive thoughts can help. The poems *The Wishing Well* and *Walking Back To Happiness* describe how to visualise those positive thoughts for the good of the planet.

During October 2019, the debates and negotiations concerning Brexit were getting really heated and nobody could agree on anything. I found it hard to understand why the different parties involved in running our country couldn't agree to work together, for the good of the nation and the world in general.

One night while all this was going on, I had a dream that the stars were twinkling hope. I woke up in the dark and thought that I should write something down, but I was too lazy to get out of bed!

In the morning, the words were still in my mind and I wrote the poem *The Stars That Twinkled Hope.* Eventually, there would be twelve poems all about working together as a team for the good of planet Earth and our future generations.

When the Covid-19 virus arrived and we went into "lockdown" I wrote the poem *Has God Gone On Holiday?* I couldn't believe after all the twinkling, beaming and shining from the Moon and Mars, The Twinkling Stars and The Sun, something so catastrophic could be upon us.

Of course, God came right back from his holiday to help and get things in order and I went on to write more poems encouraging working together during the pandemic. I always try to keep the poems cheerful and comforting.

These poems were very popular, from The Twinkling Stars, Jupiter's Disco Boots, Lovely Venus and of course Mother Nature. Everyone was uplifted by their stories.

The Government's intention when putting the country into "lockdown" was to save the NHS from becoming overwhelmed.

When all the schools, shops, pubs, cafes, restaurants and leisure centres were closed in March 2020, some people began to "panic buy" in the supermarkets. Pasta, baked beans and specifically toilet rolls began to disappear off the shelves.

We were asked not to go out of our homes, only for exercise and food shopping. We were not supposed to meet up with family or friends. No hugging or standing less than two metres apart.

Amazingly, the weather during this first "lockdown" was superb. People could walk in the parks and sunbathe in their gardens. Aeroplanes were grounded and no one was travelling into the city, so the air quality improved and people slowed down and started to appreciate nature again. After a few weeks of wandering the streets on my own for exercise and not hugging my family, I wrote the poem *A Freedom Money Can't Buy.*

One day I went on a frenzied mission down to the local shops for a loaf of bread. I was wearing an oversized hand-made face mask and the whole journey was like an episode of Mission Impossible! That evening I wrote the poem *Lockdown Shopping.*

Every day on the News there was a fresh problem and people across the globe were finding it difficult to sleep at night, especially those who weren't lucky enough to have a garden or had lost their jobs and had families to feed. I wrote a poem called *Help Is At Hand.* The sharks and crocodiles being all the different issues and just when you thought one problem was solved, another one popped up!

A favourite poem which touched people's hearts regarding not being able to sleep at night was *The Angels Bring Love And Light Into My Troubled Lockdown Night.* I wanted to let people know Angels really are very close to us at this unprecedented time in history. As we came out of one "lockdown" and eventually found ourselves experiencing a second, I sent out uplifting poems to friends and family every couple of weeks, sometimes more frequently.

One day in late September 2020 I noticed my next door neighbours had bought some enchanting fairy figures and put them under a large tree in their front garden and I couldn't resist writing the poem *Do You Believe In Fairies?* It was easy to imagine the tiny fairies sending love to the humans as they walked down our street during their "lockdown" exercise.

The fairies also gave comfort to people who couldn't sleep at night, overwhelmed with world events and political arguments. I particularly love the words to the poem *A Fairy Lullaby.* "Don't be afraid. Be calm be still. Love will find a way and always will."

The Dragon poems came from different beginnings. After I finished *The Stars That Twinkled Hope* poems, I decided to write something for my sister's grandchildren, just for them and just for fun. So I wrote *The Pink Dragon* and the children enjoyed the poem so much, I wrote a few more for them and for friend's grandchildren, writing a bespoke story for each family.

My sister Lesley was inspired by the Dragon poems and wrote a couple for her grandchildren and my nephew's wife Katie Swire wrote *The Rainbow Dragon.*

It was fantastic to have all these poems about colourful Dragons and I thought I would put them all in this book and include them in the quest to heal planet Earth.

I decided The Rainbow Dragon would lead all the colourful dragons upon the quest and somehow, Puff, a dragon full to bursting with magic, appeared as his trusted friend.

The Dragon poems bring attention to the realisation that young people today, all over the world, are working together to heal planet Earth. I believe many highly evolved souls are being born at this unprecedented time and they bring with them solutions to the problems our planet faces today. How exciting is that!

As all these sparkling words were flowing from my pen, I was also receiving poems through email and the post, composed by more family and friends, who have been inspired to write poetry themselves, after reading my books and poems. I have been really thrilled to receive so many funny, emotional, thoughtful and uplifting poems during these last couple of years and I asked each poet if they would mind me using their work in this book. After taking some time to eat delicious cake, they kindly gave their permission!

After we came out of the second "lockdown" in April 2021, my head was buzzing again with the fast pace of the twenty-first century. My flow of creativity stopped for awhile, until I wrote the poem, *The Cosmic Queue of Love.*

I then went on to write the last few poems in the book, which are about one of my favourite subjects, The Universe. I believe everything in the Universe is connected, the birds, bees, flowers, trees, animals, people, mountains and seas. The planets and the stars are especially important to the welfare of the whole magnificent Universe.

Even though we are all connected as one, we are at the same time, individuals, unique and special.

I have also included in this book, Jessica's wonderful poem *Up In Space,* which she wrote during her early years in secondary school.

I believe Jessica and the Angels encouraged those stars to twinkle hope into my mind on that special night in October 2019 and it was then The Cosmic Quest To Heal Planet Earth really began!

The Cosmic Quest

To Heal

Planet Earth

Peace on Earth – Our Future

John Lennon said "Imagine"
and I believe the time is near,
when man will love
his fellow man and all
religions will disappear.

The truth, that we are all the same,
made of cosmic energy.
One day will be a knowledge,
received with joy
and clear for all to see!

Until that day,
we have to strive to care
for one another.
Look at every living being,
as if they are your brother.

We must not forget
the plants and animals,
who share our precious planet.
Responsibility rests with human beings,
for the special things that live upon it.

So, be strong, be wise.
Don't just think of "now".
The next generation are our future.
May their thoughts of us
begin with wow!

Angela
Composed in 2017

A Whisper On The Breeze

I'm amazed how much I understand.
Amazed how much I see,
the beauty in the colours
Nature's love has shown to me.

Each flower, bird and animal
the insects and the trees,
are telling me they love me,
through a whisper on the breeze.

I feel their joy in living.
I know their love is true.
So when they ask me for my help,
I know what I must do.

They implore that we try harder,
to keep our planet safe.
So all of Nature's creatures
can thrive in this lovely place.

Please say a prayer when you awake,
that we will find a way,
of helping Nature flourish
and together, we'll save the day!

Composed by Angela
May 2019

The Wishing Well

I have a wonderful secret,
but believe it's time to tell.
I've found a very special place,
where sits a Wishing Well.

It's Mother Nature's gift to man,
somewhere to share our dreams.
Lovingly placed within our hearts.
(I think you know what I mean.)

I like to go there when I can
and wish away for hours.
I ask for rainbows, peace and love
and very soon, these precious gifts could be ours.

Try it!

Angela
March 2020

With millions of sparkles!

Walking Back To Happiness

Did you know if YOU imagine,
our world embraced by peace.
The fighting and indecisions
will slowly start to cease.

The world will be a glorious place,
where every living thing will thrive.
We'll all be dancing in the streets,
maybe attempt the jive.

So FOCUS on our world at peace
and we will start to believe.
And those fabulous words from the sixties
will give us the boost that we need.

Walking Back To Happiness
Woopah Oh Yeah Yeah!

Angela
21st April 2020

Let's Dance!

11

A Cosmic Rough And Tumble

Although it seems like chaos looms
don't be misunderstood.
The rough and tumble we're going through
will produce positive change,
for the good.

Just like a cosmic washing machine,
we're being churned round and round.
Up and down and inside out,
no care for where we're bound

But, when the cycle is finished
and the Earth comes to her
well earned rest.
Be assured this rough and tumble
will have been for our very best!

Angela
5th May 2020

We can beat the suds!

The Angel Of The Earth

There is an angel
so vast, so strong.
She holds our world
in the palms of her hands.

Her mighty wings
surround our planet,
from snowy mountains
to hot desert sands.

As she looks down
she hears us calling
and a smile lights
up her face.

She blows love
all over our planet.
Her wish?
To heal the human race.

Angela
20th May 2020

The Stars That

Twinkled Hope

And The Heavenly

Team

The Stars That Twinkled Hope

Looking down on Earth one day,
from her lofty place in space.
The star called Hope looked worried
and the smile disappeared from her face.

The planet Earth, so blue, so green,
was looking rather sad.
The little star had never seen
her colours quite so bad.

What can I do to help the Earth?
The kind star frowned – then – Yes!
I'll ask my loving fellow stars
to join me in what we do best!

From the corners of the Universe,
the stars all came together
and twinkled hope around the Earth,
to help the planet get better!

Thank you so much, said the little star
and embraced her friends with love.
We've helped the Earth together,
with our friendship from above.

Angela
31st October 2019
Composed with hopefulness and twinkles!

The Moon Beams Hope and Love

The sleepy moon awoke and
shook and shivered with delight.
Something very special was about to happen
on this night!

He knew the stars were twinkling hope
around the mighty Earth below.
He really wanted to give his help,
so decided to have a go!

From behind dark clouds very slowly,
appeared his smiling face
and he sent down lots of love and hope
to embrace the human race.

How pleased he was to give his love
and help the Earth below.
He decided to bring his friend called Mars
and encourage him to have a go!

When the Moon and Mars and the twinkling Stars
came together for the force of good,
the people on Earth all smiled,
to show they understood.

Angela
8th November 2019
With lots of love and moon beams!

The Day The Sun Shone
Hope, Love And Peace

The lazy Sun reached for a glass
of ice cold lemonade.
She was feeling so much hotter
than she used to, nowadays.

I think I need a comforting breeze
of chilly mountain air.
I'll get a little closer to the snow caps,
if I dare.

Hold on a minute, I think I can hear a call.
It's the Moon and Mars and
the Twinkling Stars.
I'll hang about here after all.

They're asking me to help them
in their quest to heal the world.
I think I'd better join them.
There's still life in this old girl!

So, the Moon and Mars, the Twinkling Stars
and the Sun, all joined together.
In, hope, peace and love, which they
sent down from above.
And our precious Earth, began to get better!

Angela
16th November 2019

And the people all sang Amen!

18

The Heart Of Mother Earth

I can feel there's something stirring
within the heart of Mother Earth.
She's shaking and she's shifting,
giving it all she's worth!

With the Moon and Mars, the twinkling Stars
and the Sun sending hope from above.
She is starting to feel a new beginning is real
and she is tingling with the strength of their love.

It's now time for us to change, no more causing her pain.
Let us all embrace the Earth with a cuddle.
If we can do this, our precious Earth will feel bliss
and we'll help her rise out of this muddle.

Let's begin!

Angela
13th February 2020
With lots of love and light!

Is God On Holiday?

God was away on holiday
when the emergency call came through.
It was the Moon and Mars,
the Twinkling Stars and the Sun
all wondering what to do.

"The humans on Earth are in a terrible state
and need to receive God's support."
They were sorry to disturb him,
as he'd just reached for a glass of port!

"Stay calm my friends." God said with love
and he licked his lips and had a think.
"I don't believe this is quite the
time for me to have that drink."

"You must ask the Angels
to sing their Song of Hope.
Embrace each and every one on earth
and this will help them cope."

"Oh thank you God,
we knew that you would know just what to do.
We'll call out to the Angels
and their sparkling love, will see us through."

Angela
April 2020

I'm sure God is on his way home now!

God Is Coming Home

"Now I've had the call, I had better not stall.
Although I've enjoyed this Heavenly Spa!
The people on Earth all need me.
I'll cadge a lift from a Shooting Star."

Meanwhile the Angels were spreading their wings
and sparkling all over the world.
The people had started to smile again.
The Song of Hope tune was doing very well!

Then God arrived home in a shower of sparks
from the speed of the Shooting Star.
"Thank you, kind friend, for bringing me home.
There is work to be done here for sure."

So, God, the Angels and the Heavenly Team,
set to work in healing the world.
In times like these it's best to pull together
and so much love will begin to unfurl.

Angela
17th April 2020

Many a truth was spoken with a twinkle!

The Angels Song Of Love

The Moon and Mars, the Twinkling Stars
and the Sun had been doing their best,
twinkling, beaming and shining
and now they needed a rest.

They sat in the shade of a leafy glade
and munched on fruit from the trees.
They were blessed to be refreshed,
from all their hard work,
by the breath of a clean, cool, breeze.

"Do you think those Angels are doing their bit
by singing that Hopeful tune?"
Mars had the hump, as he was working so hard
and he addressed this to his friend, the Moon.

"Just because you can't see them, doesn't mean they're not there.
They are sparkling and singing their tune.
The whole world will feel better from the sound of their love
and this will start to happen, very soon."

By now Mars was snoozing.
The Twinkling Stars had quit jawing and the Sun
was starting to doze.
The Moon lifted his head and looking upwards he said
"I believe it is time for this Heavenly team
to go to bed!"

Angela
24th April 2020

God's Heavenly Team Rise Again

The Moon and Mars, the Twinkling Stars and the Sun
woke up, at the sound of God's voice.
"I'm sorry to disturb you, dear friends,
but I'm afraid I have no choice."

"Some people on Earth aren't listening,
to the Song of Hope and all that stuff.
And the Angel of the Earth is getting tired.
She's running out of puff!"

So the Moon and Mars, the Twinkling Stars and the Sun
all rushed to get dressed.
They couldn't stay in their PJs.
They simply had to look their best.

Up and dressed and good to go
the Heavenly Team addressed their leader.
"We'll help you God in any way we can,
but this quest's not getting any easier."

"I know my friends, we may indeed
need extra help one day,
but for now let's give it all we've got.
What do you say?"

The Moon and Mars the Twinkling Stars and the Sun
linked hands together
and with no sign of hesitation said
"Your Team will all support you God,
today, tomorrow and forever!"

Angela
4th June 2020

The Day Jupiter Arrived On The Bus

The Moon, Mars, The Twinkling Stars
The Sun and God were puzzled.
So much love was reaching the planet,
yet the people were still very muddled.

They were running and jumping, shouting and calling,
but no one was actually listening.
They were so intent on their rushing around
they couldn't see the Stars all glistening.

So, the Twinkling Stars whispered to Mars
"Who do you think God will Zoom in to help us?"
Mars scratched his chin, on his face a big grin.
"I hear Jupiter is catching the night bus."

The Sun and the Moon who were singing a tune
heard that Jupiter was well on his way.
They all sung and danced, as this was another chance
to finally save the day!

Angela
27th July 2020

Cos we're singing a happy song!

The Day God Switched On His Disco Ball

Jupiter was wearing disco boots
when he stepped down from the bus.
He'd been having such a fabulous time,
but when God asked him to come and help,
he knew he simply must.

His friends all crowded round him,
admiring his sparkly shoes.
Then they all sat down together
for tea and toast and to share their news.

"So, the people on Earth aren't listening
to all your happy songs.
The Moon's beaming and the Sun's shining,
but the people still keep getting it wrong?"

"What more can we do?" cried The Twinkling Stars
still amazed at Jupiter's disco gear.
"I think we've got to sing much louder,
so the people on Earth start to cheer."

The Sun was shining brightly,
she had something exciting to say.
"Let's ask God to lend us his Disco Ball.
That would surely save the day."

So, God's Disco Ball started sparkling, its
rays reaching all over the world.
The people all started to clap and cheer
and the Angels watched the goodness unfurl.
I will survive, I will survive. Oh Yeah!!

Angela
18th August 2020

The Day Venus Helped The Heavenly Team

Venus was having her hair done
when Pluto dropped by for a chat.
They usually talked about love and stuff,
but especially this and that!

"Have you heard the clapping and cheering
and seen the dancing to God's Disco Ball?
The people on Earth seem happy.
They're determined to make the best of it all."

Venus walked slowly away from the mirror.
She generally felt she looked good.
A lovely glow shone all around her
and she smiled, as Pluto knew she would.

"The people on Earth are mostly strong and wise
and yes, I can hear them singing "I will survive!"
The Heavenly Team are doing their very best.
I'll offer to help, so they can have a rest."

So, Venus stepped in
to give the Heavenly Team a break.
She knew her nails needed doing
but that would have to wait!

Angela
24th August 2020

Mother Nature's Wise Words

Mother Nature watched,
in quiet contemplation, whilst
the Heavenly Team were doing their best
for each and every nation.

First the Twinkling Stars had gathered,
with the help of the lovely Moon.
Then grumpy Mars had joined the Team,
but wanted to go home soon!

That great "hot" lady the Sun
did her best.
Shining and sweating
all over the rest.

Jupiter danced his way
through the crowd.
To encourage the people to sing
very loud.

Beautiful Venus took her time to ensure,
the Team had their rest
before she was
pampered some more!

Little Pluto watched Venus,
his eyes all a glow.
He was madly in love with her,
but hoped it didn't show.

God loved this Team and gave
everyone his full support.
So, Mother Nature closed her eyes.
It was time to give this some thought.

"It seems the Team have understood,
to heal the Earth, we need to work together.
When with respect, we embrace our differences,
most things turn out for the better."

Then from way up high
within the Milky Way,
sparkles began to peep!
And wise old Mother Nature
lay her head down for a sleep.

Angela
3rd September 2020

And so it is.

"Lockdown"

Rhymes

How Lucky Am I

How lucky am I
to roam free on my bike.
To walk in the hills
on a long summer's hike.

To sit on a bench
in the shade of a tree
and listen to the birds
sing their sweet songs to me.

I look up at blue sky
and white fluffy clouds.
A sight I could stay
and gaze at for hours.

How splendid is life
when you're healthy and free.
I realise how precious
these moments should be.

Take your time to enjoy
the special gifts that you've got,
as in the blink of an eye
they could be gifts you have not.

Angela

Originally composed in June 2017
Last verse rewritten in November 2020

A Freedom
Money Can't Buy

Now I've had time to sit awhile
and wonder what I miss.
The things that money can buy
are not at the top of my list.

Maybe a plate of baked beans on toast
or pasta with a little cheese.
Toilet rolls, piled high in the loo.
Perhaps I could do, with some of these.

I think I will cope
when my legs get hairy.
Then my eyebrows need a trim
and my roots get scary.

But freedom to walk out of my front door,
ready to start a new day.
And freedom to hug the people I love,
is what I'll miss now that's taken away.

Angela
March 2020

But not for long!
Think of all that hugging to come!

Heather's Cake

Another day in "lockdown"
I was in my kitchen preparing lunch,
when I thought I heard the doorbell ring
and I had a hunch.

Could this be the postman
with a letter from my friend.
Or the parcel I've been waiting for
which has been driving me round the bend!

No! It's Heather with a fantastic cake
she has baked with love for us all.
It really tastes delicious and I must thank her
with a special call.

Thank you Heather

A kind neighbour with a generous heart.

Angela
13th May 2020

Lockdown Shopping

Today I am walking to the shops
trying the best I can,
ducking and diving and crossing the road,
to avoid my "brotherhood of man."

I was wearing a mask I made all by myself,
as big as a dustbin lid.
It wasn't just my nose and mouth
this monster actually hid.

I couldn't breathe and couldn't see
my purse when I went to pay.
I think I'll have to try a new design
for another day.

Outside the shop, I ripped free of the mask
and zigzagged my way back home.
I think it will be at least a week
before I decide again to roam!

Angela
14th May 2020

Learning new skills!

Forever in PJs

Hey, did I just hear we're
easing out of "lockdown"?
I was so surprised when I got the call,
I actually slammed the phone down.

What a shock, I must confess,
this means I'll probably
have to get dressed!

It feels like a life time
I've been stuck here in the house.
Comfy in my PJs
and never going out.

I suppose I had better start thinking ahead.
No, hold on a minute.
I think, I'll just jump back into bed!

Angela
13th May 2020

Rainbows Love Different Colours

Rainbows are a bunch of different colours,
shining for a common good.
Deep dark reds, pale yellows and blues.
I can't keep count of the
many varied hues.

If only we could work in harmony down here.
Respect and enjoy our differences.
Give everyone a hug and sometimes
even share a beer.

For in the end the truth is clear,
we're all of value on this sphere.
So love thy neighbour
whenever differences appear
and get down to the pub for that ice cold beer!

Angela
10th June 2020

Don't all rush to the bar!

Help Is At Hand

I had another dream last night
and the dream I dreamt
gave me a fright.

I was swimming through a choppy sea
and hungry sharks
were chasing me!

I could see the safety of the beach,
but it always seemed
just out of reach.

And when I thought I'd made it through,
a crocodile popped up
and shouted "Boo!"

I decided to think of calming thoughts
to get me to the beach
of course.

So I swam serenely through that choppy sea,
in my shark proof bubble
and that saved me.

I landed safely on the sand
and knew I'd had
a helping hand.

Angela
30th June 2020

The Flame Of Hope

I know I should be merry
at this Christmas time of year.
But these past few months have been
a time of much sorrow
and great fear.

I feel I'm overwhelmed with thoughts
that just won't let me smile.
I think I'll go and sit down
beside the fire for a little while.

As I sip my cocoa
and look into the flames.
I start to feel so much better.
Even cheerful once again!

Suddenly I'm hopeful.
I light some candles as I'm filled with love.
"Light will always banish darkness."
Sang the Angels, from somewhere up above.

Angela
28th December 2020

The flame of hope will never go out.
Even when it gets blown about!

Our Changing Times

The times they are a changing,
but I'm sure things will turn out for the best.
Right now we're all in confusion
and the many rules are anybody's guess.

One day I can go inside a café,
sit down with a friend and have tea.
The next day I'm outside and I'm freezing.
No one is allowed indoors with me!

The rules are meant to keep us healthy
and I'm focusing on their good intent.
But all over the United Kingdom,
these health saving rules are definitely getting bent.

In the future we'll look back at this time
and say we found it a bit of a mess.
"But did you try and do your best during those difficult days?"
I believe you'll be able to say "Yes."

Angela
4th January 2021

Can someone just explain the rules to me again?

A Happy Place

It's hard to stay calm and focused.
This is not an easy ride.
Sometimes it becomes a struggle,
as though we're swimming against the tide.

I know it will be worth it.
We'll get there in the end.
We'll navigate those huge great waves.
Those twists and turns and bends.

We'll come out on the other side
and the world will be a happier place.
The sun will always be shining
and we'll have great big smiles on our face!

Angela
9th January 2021

Snorkels and flippers at the ready!

The Angels Bring Love And Light
Into My Troubled Lockdown Night

I wake up suddenly in the dark of the night,
my thoughts so sad and my chest feeling tight.
I call out. "Someone help me!" But I don't hear a reply.
I lay back on my pillows and quietly begin to cry.

Then very, very softly
I feel a hand upon my cheek
and then a sense of warmth and love
gives me the comfort that I seek.

"Dear precious child of the Universe
we are here as loving Guides,
to remind you of the inner strength
your heart holds deep inside."

"Remember Angels are always near,
to hold your hand and take away your fear.
So, settle down and go to sleep.
We'll stay here beside you, till the morning light
through the window peeps."

Angela
6th February 2021

Remember Angels are always near.
Don't forget.

**Inspired To Write
In The Angels Tender Loving Light**

Great News!
Lockdown rules have changed and
I can dream of embracing
my loved ones again.

As I slept I heard a plea.
Angels were quietly calling to me.
I rubbed my eyes and scratched my head
and saw the light of loving Angels around my bed.

"The people of the Earth
have been given some time
to slow down, take a rest
and ease their minds."

"Please don't rush back
to thoughtless grind.
To your wondrous Planet Earth
let your hearts be kind."

I thought I'd better take some notes
and this is how the Angels spoke.
The lovely light around my bed, disappeared
and I went back to scratching my head.

Angela
24th February 2021

We'll have to give this some thought.

When You're Smiling

How you doing?
I think I'm doing well.
Of course, really,
only time will tell.

I've had one jab and
got another one to come.
At least they don't need to
stick it in my bum!

Got used to me mask
and running quite fast,
when shopping in the aisles
with many "others."

The thought of a meal
amongst a crowded clientele,
now gives me a case
of the "shudders."

But soon will come the day,
I can throw my mask away.
(No, recycle, recycle.)
And start planning ahead for
my holiday.

So, keep on smiling.
Cos when you're smiling
the whole world smiles with you!

Angela
6th March 2021

Freedom From Lockdown At Last

Now I'm free to roam around,
meet with friends, go into town.
Book a holiday, but not sure where,
as they tell us we should still take care.

My head is truly buzzing
with all the things I now CAN do.
And I'm bursting with excitement,
as I've just had jab number two!

But, we really must remember,
in the " release from lockdown" rush,
to still take time for quiet
and a little bit of hush.

Remember our precious Planet Earth
and all the people who dwell around her.
Take thoughtful steps to help her thrive,
and she'll reward us with Nature's wonder.

Angela
30th April 2021

Small thoughtful changes can make a big difference!

Do You Believe

In Fairies?

Do You Believe In Fairies?

There are fairies amongst the flowers
in the house next door to me.
They live in the front garden,
under a shady tree.

Just like that Old Woman
they live happily in a shoe,
but these pretty little fairies
know just what to do.

They look after all the humans
who take a walk along the street,
by smiling and waving,
their thoughts so very sweet.

They will offer you some fairy tea
in a great big china cup.
Then sit right down beside you
and take great joy in watching you sup.

Soon you'll hear their laughter,
as they play on their swings and dance in the dew.
A display that is very precious,
as it shows their love for you.

So, if you walk along this road
and you may be feeling sad.
Just look for these little fairies
and your heart will start to feel glad!

Angela
24th September 2020

A Fairy Adventure

Last night in bed I tossed and turned
and couldn't get to sleep.
These crazy days were playing on my mind
and I was about to weep.

But just as I reached out
to get a tissue for my nose.
A little fairy hand began
to tickle my feet and toes.

Then I felt a gentle fairy hand upon my head
and suddenly there were lots of tiny fairies
jumping up and down upon my bed!

"Everything will work out well,
this is no time to weep.
Big change equals adventure.
We'll give you a cuddle to help you sleep."

I woke up in the morning strong
and ready to face the day.
I looked around for my fairy friends,
but they had all gone away.

I hope that they will come again
if I am feeling lost and low.
But right now I'm up for an adventure.
Come on everybody, let's go!

Angela
14th October 2020

A Fairy Lullaby

I lay awake in the dark of the night,
thinking that life is getting scary!
My mouth felt dry and my heart was pounding.
Where were those little fairies?

Then from the corner of my eye
I glimpsed a glow of light.
A tiny Fairy Prince appeared and said
"We will stay with you this night."

He climbed upon my pillow
and sat down close to me.
Then he clapped his little fairy hands
and I was amazed to see ....

A tiny fairy orchestra
alight upon my bed
and play a soothing lullaby
to rest my heart and head.

"Don't be afraid.
Be calm and still.
Love will find a way
and always will."

Then I think I fell asleep
and presently began to snore.
And those lovely little fairies
tiptoed out the door!

Angela
16th October 2020

A Fairy Wedding

I was out in the garden
digging up some weeds.
The wind was blowing gently
and I looked up at the trees.

The reds, the golds and yellows of the
rustling, glistening leaves,
made me feel so very happy
and put my mind at ease.

Then I thought I heard the tinkling clink
of glasses raised in a toast.
I peeked into next door's garden
and I spied a fairy host.

It was a Fairy Wedding.
The Prince had found his bride.
There were hundreds of tiny fairies.
No Covid rules for them abide.

The bride and groom were
standing on a mushroom looking pleased.
There was so much fairy dust about
I had to try hard not to sneeze!

I quietly turned back to my garden
with a great big smile on my face.
I left the wedding party in peace
as they cut the Fairy Cake.

Angela
20th October 2020

Mmmmmm - cake!

51

A Fairy Cake

I tossed and turned in bed last night
and broke out in a sweat.
Crazy thoughts wouldn't let me sleep.
I had my worst night yet.

I sat up, tense and looked around
for someone to help me out.
Then I heard the sound of little fairies
begin to call and shout.

I looked down towards their voices
and right beside my bed was a long line of fairies,
passing a huge slice of fairy cake
above their tiny heads!

"We've brought you some Fairy Wedding Cake
to help you fall asleep.
Working together as a team we've carried it from Fairyland,
to bring you some night time peace."

As I lay back and scoffed the cake
I felt love for this fairy band.
And I wondered if they had more scrumptious cake,
in this place called Fairyland?

Angela
23rd October 2020

So much happiness evolves from the baking and eating of cake!

The Grumpy Fairy

I looked out of the window
and the clouds had blown away.
So I decided to put my washing out
on this sunny Autumn day.

As I was pegging hubby's socks
upon the washing line.
I heard the sound of tiny voices
and one was getting out of line.

"I'm fed up with these humans,
they can't seem to get things right.
They're confused by ever changing rules
and everyone's up for a fight!"

Two little fairies sat nearby
on an upturned flower pot.
One looked really grumpy
and happily the other one did not.

"You're always grumpy nowadays,
you need to take a break.
These poor humans are feeling sad
and their hearts are bound to ache."

"We need to help the people smile.
So stop your grumpy moaning.
Let's take a bag of Fairy Dust
and we will go a roaming."

So, the Grumpy Fairy and his kind friend
sprinkled Fairy Dust far and wide.
Then all the people started to smile
and feel a little better deep inside.

Angela
8th November 2020
I am the Grumpy Fairy. Where's that Fairy Dust?

The Grumpy Fairy Smiles Again

As the Grumpy Fairy and his kind friend
sprinkled Fairy Dust
all over the land.
Hundreds of tiny fairies came to help,
from the place called Fairyland.

Soon the humans who had begun to smile,
slowed down to rest and feel happy for a while.
They started to imagine Fairyland,
where people worked together
to give Mother Nature a helping hand.

No cars and great long traffic queues.
No noisy alarm clocks too.
Just buzzing bees and bird song
and time to really live.
The fairies were doing a brilliant job.
They had so much love to give.

Suddenly, the Grumpy Fairy wasn't grumpy anymore.
He felt so much better with every smiling human that he saw.
When all the lovely fairies felt they'd given the world a hand,
they flew in a cloud of sparkling wings,
back home to Fairyland.

Angela
16th November 2020

Wait for me sparkly fairies! I'm coming to Fairyland!

A Fairy Christmas 2020

Soon it will be Christmas time.
The year 2020!
These past few months have been so difficult.
We could do with cheer a plenty.

Inside a crackling fire glows
on this frosty Winter's eve.
And the lights upon the Christmas tree
twinkle and shine, not just for me!

What's that I hear? A tiny baby's cry
and a whispered reassurance, from a mother filled with love.
Something very special has occurred,
under the shining stars above.

I peek beneath the Christmas tree
and can't believe my eyes.
A tiny Fairy Reindeer's Sleigh
has come from the star filled skies.

And on that Sleigh a tiny baby Fairy lies
snuggled in blankets, warm and cosy.
I have to take a closer look,
as I am very nosy.

It is the Fairy Prince and as I remember,
his lovely bride.
They are looking at their Fairy baby
with so much love and pride.

Let's celebrate this Christmas
with mistletoe and wine.
And hope this little baby's birth,
will help the Earth to shine!

Angela
1st December 2020
And the bells jingled loudly all over the world!

Fairy Wishes Just For You

The fairies in the garden
were very sleepy and content.
They had been playing, smiling
and waving at the humans.
Now all their fairy energy was spent.

Christmas time had been lots of fun.
The sparkling lights were extremely uplifting.
Santa's jolly Reindeers had decided to come along,
pulling Santa's Sleigh with precious gifts in.

Now that Christmas time was over,
how could they encourage the humans to smile?
The fairies put the kettle on
and sat down to have a think for a while.

They heard the sound of bird song
and the squirrels chattering to each other.
Then they looked up into the branches of the tree,
whose leaves would soon give them much needed cover.

"Why, Mother Nature will bring a smile to their faces,
as they see all the green shoots of Spring.
And we will help the people have hope,
as we continue to dance and sing!"

Angela
January 2021

And the fairies began to dance just for you.

A Fairy Celebration

I heard the message loud and clear.
"The end of lockdown is nearly here!"
Then from next door the sound of fairy cheer,
whilst drinking lots of delicious beer.

As you know, I don't usually pry.
But I spotted a hole in the fence from which to spy.
The tiny creatures were having such fun.
Even handing round some Good Fairy rum.

"Let's hope our lovely humans
will take this second chance,
to give kindness to the planet Earth,
then we will sing and dance!"

I stepped back from my peephole
and went inside to make my tea.
Surely we, as humans, will take this second chance.
Make the fairies really proud of us.
Then yes, altogether, we'll sing and dance!

Angela
14th March 2021

A little kindness goes a long way.

Do You Believe

In Dragons?

Do You Believe In Dragons?

The huge and friendly dragon awoke,
in his cosy mountain lair.
"I think I'll do some Christmas shopping."
Now for a dragon this is rare!

He thought that he should clean his teeth
and wash behind his ears.
He knew he should look his very best,
as he hadn't been out for years.

While he cooked a hearty breakfast,
he pondered on why he was awake.
Dragons usually stay in bed
when humans eat Christmas cake.

Suddenly he realised
what he was meant to do.
Bring lots of fun and sunny smiles
to all the little children that he knew.

This was the Rainbow Dragon
and he thundered from the cave with glee.
He was off to ask his friend called Puff to help
and he lived down by the sea.

Puff was just magic and said he'd help
the children smile,
together with lots of other dragons,
who'd been asleep for a long, long while.

Angela
5th December 2020

The Dragons New Year Quest

The Rainbow Dragon and his good friend Puff
flew up and away from the sea.
Higher and higher above the forests and mountains,
as high as a Dragon can be!

Then they called, as only a Dragon can call,
to awaken their colourful friends.
And one by one the mighty Dragons awoke,
to give their help to the world once again.

"There's very important work to be done,
but we'll still have time to have lots of fun!
We must encourage young humans to do their very best,
in this year 2021 when they begin their new Quest."

"They know what is right
and will try with all their might,
with their new ideas and brilliant solutions
to make the future bright."

So, in a perfect puff of magic
the Dragons rose up and flew away.
Then all the little children smiled
and looked forward to Happy Days!

Angela
1st January 2021

The future's looking bright! Where are those sunglasses?

The Pink Dragon

Theo, Zoe, Charlie and Max went down to the woods to play.
Their nanny and granddad had packed them
a wonderful lunch and waved,
calling "Have a great day."

Theo and Max led the way
through the trees.
They'd never seen such tall ones,
with big shiny leaves.

Zoe and Charlie were
ambling along,
looking for rabbits
and singing a song.

Then suddenly from somewhere
hidden by the long grass, came the
sound of a baby
who had started to laugh.

The children edged forward
and parted the reeds.
There on a toadstool sat baby Lyra,
well pleased.

"Oh, how did you get here?"
The children asked in surprise.
"My friend the Pink Dragon brought me,
from high in the skies."

As the children looked on, from the lake just beyond,
rose a Dragon, a deep shade of pink.
She flew high in the sky and as she passed them by,
she gave them a cheeky wink!

Composed by Aunty Angela
For Theo, Max, Zoe, Charlie and Lyra
April 2020

The Blue Dragon

Theo, Zoe and Lyra
were on their way to the park.
They were meeting their cousins, Charlie and Max
and had been told
"Come home before it gets dark."

Zoe was pushing the buggy
with baby Lyra snuggled inside
and Theo was carrying the backpack,
filled with lemonade, crisps
and pork pies.

Suddenly they spotted Charlie and Max
at the top of a huge slippery slide.
They were getting ready
to whiz down together.
What a fantastic ride!

"Hurry up Zoe." cried Theo,
as he ran to join in the fun.
"Be as fast as you can Zoe,
I think that you'd better run."

Zoe looked on
at the boys having fun,
but because of the buggy
she certainly couldn't run.

Then down from the clouds
came a Dragon so blue.
He was smiling and laughing
as towards them
he flew.

"Jump up on my back girls.
I'll take you two for a ride,
which you'll never forget
for the rest of your lives!"

The girls flew with the Blue Dragon,
all over the park
and the boys shouted from below.
"Hey girls, remember,
we must be home before dark!"

Composed by Aunty Angela
For

Theo, Zoe, Max, Charlie
and Lyra

1st May 2020

The Purple Dragon

Today the cousins were down on the beach
playing in the sand.
When suddenly Theo shouted " LOOK
there is a great big Purple Dragon
about to land!"

Max looked over and said with a grin.
"Come and play with us.
Help us dig."
"Actually said the Dragon,
I think I am too big!"

So Charlie said in a very loud voice.
"Would you like to sit and have a drink?"
"Mmmm" said the Dragon, "It's the same colour as me!
I will have to have a think!"

Zoe ran down to the sea
and jumped in a foamy wave.
The Dragon said "I don't like the sea,
I think you are very brave."

"I like to be there, in the blue
with the clouds up high.
Jump on my back cousins
and we will fly up to the sky."

Holding onto baby Lyra,
they climbed onto the Dragon
and held on tight.
The dragon flew up and up
till the beach was out of sight!

65

They flew over all the land
then said, "We must be back for tea."
They looked far down below them and saw
Nanny and Granddad's bungalow
by the sea!!

Composed by Nanny Lesley

For
Theo, Zeo, Max, Charlie
And Lyra

4th May 2020

The Yellow Dragon

It was a lovely blue sky day
and the cousins were ready to have some fun.
They ran along the path, down to the lake
and out into the sun.

They stopped on a bridge to feed the ducks.
Max said "In my pocket I have some bread."
Then they heard a voice say
"I'm hungry can you feed me instead?"

They turned to see the little Yellow Dragon,
coming out from behind a tree.
He said "I can't find my family.
I think they have forgotten me."

Zoe said "We will help you find them."
Charlie took his hand and led him to the green.
They laughed and played and cheered him up.
He was much happier than he had been!

Theo said "Look over there." They could see
three more dragons, searching around the ground.
"Come on little dragon
your family we have found."

They all ran together, baby Lyra on Theo's back.
"Come on little dragon" they shouted "This way."
The dragon family greeted them
with a HIP HIP HOORAY!"

Composed by Nanny Lesley
For
The cousins – May 2020

The Rainbow Dragon

Looking out of the window,
staring at the sky.
"When will we run free again?"
Said Zoe, with a sigh.

Charlie asked, "When will we see Nanny
and play outside in her garden?
Eating a cheeky ice lolly,
whilst laughing in the sun."

"When will we meet Lyra?" said Max
"And squidge her chubby cheeks.
The days are so slow in "lockdown",
it's been going on for weeks!"

"I'm bored of all this learning", said Theo,
When will it be over?
I want to go to the farm,
on holiday and to the castle in Dover."

The Rainbow Dragon heard the children
and listened to their troubles.
Don't worry he thought, I'll make you smile,
let's fill the sky with bubbles.

Lyra was the first to see
the bubbles in the air.
She looked at them intently,
and gave them a short, sharp, stare.

The children didn't see them at first,
so the dragon flew around.
Spreading the bubbles higher,
until they sank to the ground.

"Dinosaur!" said Charlie,
as he saw the bubbles pop.
"Look" said Max, pointing,
hoping they'd never stop.

"What is it?" said Theo
A superhero, I bet!"
"A Unicorn", said Zoe.
"The pink one that I met."

"It's Magic" whispered Lyra
"I've seen it here before.
If you look a little closer,
you can see it even more."

The dragon sat and watched,
floating up above.
So colourful is the rainbow
our new symbol of love.

He comes in peace, to bring us cheer.
To let the children know,
That the day will come, when we'll be one,
together for a show.

The children rushed to tell their mummy
and daddy too.
But the grown-ups couldn't see the bubbles,
they only saw the blue.

They couldn't see the bubbles,
in all their rainbow glory.
They didn't believe the children.
and laughed at their Rainbow Dragon story.

The Rainbow Dragon smiled, and flashed a toothy grin.
"I see you children, as you see me, real as we are one."
Rainbows will always be here,
if you look beyond the sun.

Composed by Katie Swire
May 2020

Inspired by Angela and Lesley

69

The Green Dragon

Ellie and Tom were walking along,
a warm breeze ruffling their hair.
When down from the sky
the Green Dragon flew by
and this gave them both quite a scare!

Tom shouted "Did you see that Ellie?
Let's run for the trees!"
But all of a sudden the huge dragon SNEEZED!
Then all around them sparkling droplets appeared.
Ellie looked at Tom and said "This is so weird."

The droplets settled on their hair and their clothes.
Their hands and their feet and the
tips of their toes.
The dragon was laughing and chuckling with glee.
"You two look so funny, will you come fly with me?"

So, Ellie and Tom jumped up high on his back,
flying through the sky, on a white fluffy track.
Up through the clouds and onwards to the stars.
Ellie said "Tom, I'm so happy, I could do this for hours."
And so they did!

Angela
5th August 2020

Composed for Ellie and Tom
The grandchildren of our friends Chris and Carol

The Red Dragon

Elsie and Joseph were down on the beach.
They were learning about fossils and who better to teach them
than Grandpa and Grandma who had been teachers in school.
They were pointing at some stones
in a little rock pool.

"How exciting children just look at this stone.
You can just see the shape of some really old bones."
Elsie and Joseph both looked down in wonder,
when suddenly they heard a noise,
which sounded like thunder!

Up on the cliff tops stood a fire breathing Red Dragon.
The warmth from his breath made Grandma put her hat on.
"Get behind me children" shouted Grandpa
"I will keep you from harm."
Then the Red Dragon smiled, with a great deal of charm.

"Don't be scared children I'm here for some fun.
I'll take you on an adventure, when your work here is done."
So, Elsie and Joseph left the old fossils on the beach
and joined the Red Dragon on his journey through the sky.
They weren't scared, just excited, but didn't know why.

The Red Dragon flew on high, until the Earth was out of reach.
The children learnt fantastic lessons
to give the "Grown Ups" they were meant to teach!

Angela
15th December 2020

Composed for Elsie and Joseph
The grandchildren of our friends Brenda and John

The Magical New Year Quest

The magnificent Rainbow Dragon
was enjoying a well earned rest.
And he spread his mighty wings to the sky
on the top of Mount Everest!

The children were smiling
and the sun really was shining.
It was a grand and bold beginning
for the Magical New Year Quest.

Puff landed beside him,
his face all a glow.
He was full to bursting with magic
and ready to go!

"Where shall we begin Rainbow
on this brand new day,
to encourage more children to be happy,
in every single way?"

"Up and away to the furthest realms a Dragon can reach.
Real love for the Planet, with your magic,
to even more children,
we will teach."

So, Puff used his magic to help the children see,
with a little love and kindness,
how truly wonderful our Planet,
would once again be.

Angela
20th January 2021

There is a little magic in all of us!

Poems Composed

By

Friends and Family

I've Just Read Your Book

I just sat down and read a book
nothing unusual you might say.
But this little book that I just read
took my breath away!

I know that it has moved me.
In a way I have to see,
if there's another poem
I can find inside of me.

I know not when I'll write it
and I know not what it's about.
But one day I hope to find a little poem
coming out.

I hope it's joyful and uplifting.
I hope for some humour too.
Before too long I hope to write a poem
again for you.

Because you lift my spirits up
with every one you send.
I plan to pen a poem to you
Angela – my friend!

Composed by Denise Rankin
September 2019

After reading Take A Walk Through My Mind.
Denise was my next door neighbour for over twenty years
and remains a good friend.

A Glimpse Of Your Childhood

The simplicity of love's recipe,
the finest ingredients at its core.
The nurturing of a family,
built on values organic and pure.

I imagine your childhood holidays
full of frolicking and laughter.
The innocence and joy abound,
a more content family portrait, never to be found.

In my mind's eye, I hear the sisters play,
I see them run in the sand.
I smell the saltiness of the sea,
I feel those memories in the eyes of my own children running free.

Your stories live on,
through my family.
A glimpse of your childhood,
replaced in my own family tree.

The happiness to be cherished.
The unity I aspire to.
The honesty to be admired.
The simplicity lives on.

Your message resonates with me,
to protect each special moment.
Live, love
and be free.

I took a walk through your mind,
to see what I could find.
I listened to your words,
so eloquent and kind.

In honour of your memories,
I smile as you pave the way.
To live each day in harmony
and be thankful come what may.

Composed by Katie Swire
July 2019

Inspired to write after reading my book
Take A Walk Through My Mind

Always There

The love we share
for those we care,
never dies,
it's always there.

And when sun shines
with clouds apart,
we think of them,
they are close to our heart.

With stars that shine
in night time skies,
love never fades
and never dies.

Composed by Pam Whittingham
13th October 2019

In memory of Jessica and passed loved ones.

Our daughters were good friends in primary school.

Posting A Letter

Out I went on a sunny afternoon
to post a letter so it would reach you soon.
I could see the post box standing still.
It was perched just at the top of the hill.
I kept on walking and to my surprise
it seemed to move further away before my eyes.
On reaching the box with its open jaw
I said "Will you deliver this to Angela to be sure."
Of course there was no reply,
but I thought I saw a winking eye!
Home I went full of glee
and made myself a cup of tea.
So with this poem I will end the day.
With lots of love it is on its way.

Composed by Uncle Roy
August 2020

My mother's eldest brother Roy,
aged eighty seven at the time of writing!

Yes I Believe In Fairies

Yes I believe in fairies
and hope they're really there.
When from my bedroom window
I sit so still and stare.

When dusk falls upon the garden
and the fox is on the prowl.
The only sound that I can hear
is from the tawny owl.

A twinkling light, a tinkling bell,
beneath the cherry tree.
Just tells me what I know is true,
there are fairies roaming free!

Composed by Joan Wilson
September 2020

Inspired by my poem *Do You Believe In Fairies?*

Joan married our cousin David and my sister and I
were bridesmaids at their wedding when we were little girls.

The Lockdown Beast

I'm so glad you're feeling well.
At last we see a way out of this hell.
A chance to meet our families and friends,
in person, not just as Zoom recommends.
With luck we might just get our holiday,
sometime soon, just not today.
Before that though, I have a lot to do.
My hair needs a cut even if I have to queue!
I must stop eating or cut back at least.
It's time to tame the Lockdown Beast!

Composed by Sarah Copeland
8th March 2021

Sarah and I have known each other
for over thirty years. She was inspired to
write the Lockdown Beast after reading
my poem *When You're Smiling.*

The Covid Haze

Rainy days,
another Lego maze.
Drifting along
in a Covid haze.

Another lockdown,
been and gone.
Home schooling meltdowns
and staying strong.

Back at school
they skip through the gate.
Who would have thought
we'd still be late!

They do not ponder
on the changes since,
our lives full of wonder
restricted to every inch.

Will they remember
the masks and the gel?
Will they tell their children
about the Coronavirus hell?

I will never forget
those long days at home.
Longing for freedom,
to get out and roam.

The tears we cried,
both happy and sad.
We tried our best,
to make good out of bad.

Alone in my thoughts
but together, we share.
Life in the pandemic.
Our bubble and only care.

Composed by Katie Swire
10th May 2021

My nephew and his wife Katie
have three children under the age of
seven and both parents worked from home
during the pandemic!

The Fabric Of Life

A coloured cloth, so rich and beautiful
is woven by skilful hands
First they fix the strong warp threads
to run long and straight and true
Then the soft weft threads flow back and forth
weaving under-over-through

The cloth is made to the rhythm
of the weavers' ancient song
And the weavers' hearts beat in time
as their dance of love flows on
until all their warps and wefts entwine
and together they all become one

This life, so rich and beautiful
is woven by unseen hands
The strong warp threads connect this world
to the stars through all of you
and we make the weft of colours
weaving under-over-through

Pink is our joy at sunrise
Blue, the peace of evening light
In summer's green we blossom and grow
then mellow when the world turns white
Fun and laughter have a golden glow
and red shows our spirit burns bright

Sorrow and tears are paler shades
their threads are made frail by pain
But the others are there to lend support
and then hope makes them strong again
So together a wonderful pattern is spun
and forever we all become One

Composed by Miriam Fraser
especially for this book
with love and wisdom
March 2021

I have known Miriam for many years
and admire her spiritual integrity. She
is a published writer herself and as you can see,
produces beautiful poetry

THE

UNIVERSE

Up In Space

Up in space there is the sun.
A big ball of fire.
Yellow, orange and red.
Melting anything that goes near it.

Up in space there is the moon.
A copper coin on a velvet background.
Bright, shining, fantastic.
Giving people light, late at night.

Up in space there are the stars.
Little fairy lights splintering the darkness.
Shooting, glistening, twinkling.
Giving people happiness.

Composed by Jessica Wignall
September 2000

Jessica wrote this poem during her early years
at secondary school.

The Cosmic Queue Of Love

Please don't despair,
they're all still there.
It's just they're finding it hard to get through.

My mind is so full
of everyday stuff
and now they're stuck in a queue!

The Stars above are full of love
and the Moon and Mars
are singing.

The red hot Sun is waiting patiently
at the back.
Her shining face is smiling, but sweating.

Venus and Pluto are filling time at the spa.
They are busy canoodling,
so we won't get far!

Jupiter has gone on a road tripping gig.
He's left word to call him
when the queue's not so big.

Here's hoping it won't take too long
to get through.
So they can bring all their sparkles and love back to you.

Angela
3rd June 2021

Peace And Love
Shine Down From Above

Today I had a thought or two,
that I should really
share with you.

To cheer you up and give you hope
and now we're free,
will help you cope.

There is a new sparkle from a tiny star.
Shining down from
ever so far.

The sparkle of love.
The sparkle of peace.
Look towards the magic
and your worries will cease.

Angela
12th May 2021

Release from "lockdown" support

The Sun And The Moon
Show Us The Way

I was snuggled deep in slumber,
when I felt the magic stir.
A tingling, glowing something,
was in the early morning air.

I stretched and pulled the covers back,
then stumbled to the door.
I slowly turned the handle and as the door
began to open, this is what I saw!

The Sun's soft rays of dawn, were shining through the windows
and had ricocheted across the hall.
Where they hit a golden sphere,
I have hung upon the wall.

An awesome glow of sunlight, lit up
and spread sparkles all around.
I felt so very humbled as I watched
Mother Nature's wondrous works abound.

The Sun was gently telling me
this was how it all began.
To wake at the touch of the Sun's tender rays
and begin the work at hand.

At the end of the day embrace healing sleep,
while the Moon shines in the dark and velvety night.
Then Mother Nature would smile and be content,
and everything would be just right!

Angela
26th June 2021

Astronomical Celebrations

The Star called Hope was planning
a celebration and she wanted to include
each and every nation.

Venus, Jupiter, little Pluto and Mars
soon received their invitations
from the Twinkling Stars.

From every corner of the Universe and deep outer space,
everyone joined together,
to celebrate with the Earth's human race.

The Moon and the Sun came from where it all begun
and they offered God a lift
so he could join in the fun!

So, every life form in the Universe,
from near and from far.
Came together in fabulous celebration
of just who we are.

The planets and the people so enjoyed the celebrations,
the day would be remembered forever
by each and every nation!

And it all started
with the love of one little Star.

Angela
26th June 2021

Author Of The Universe

Dear author of the Universe
I've read your magnificent book.
I marvel at your amazing ideas
and wonder how long it took?

I thought I'd write and let you know
how much I appreciate your endeavour.
And how I really admire you
for being extremely clever.

I feel compelled to be quite bold
and offer you my help to write the ending.
So, with that in mind I'll pick up my pen
and start on the chapters I'll be sending!

We should write about peace
and most certainly love.
I am sure the stars will help us too,
with their hopeful twinkles from above.

Angela
15th March 2021

The End

Surprise

It's not really the end!

Because the author of the Universe
will go on writing

forever

and

ever

Cosmic!

This book is about hope.
No one really knows
what the future holds for
Planet Earth.

But, as a unique
and special person,
you can help to make
the future bright.

Begin with sparkles!

Angela